ZEN
Zen for Beginners

The Ultimate Guide to Incorporating Zen into Your Life – A Zen Buddhism Approach to Happiness and Inner Peace

William Miyagi

© Copyright 2015 - All rights reserved.

In no way is it legal to reproduce, duplicate, or transmit any part of this document in either electronic means or in printed format. Recording of this publication is strictly prohibited and any storage of this document is not allowed unless with written permission from the publisher. All rights reserved.

The information provided herein is stated to be truthful and consistent, in that any liability, in terms of inattention or otherwise, by any usage or abuse of any policies, processes, or directions contained within is the solitary and utter responsibility of the recipient reader. Under no circumstances will any legal responsibility or blame be held against the publisher for any reparation, damages, or monetary loss due to the information herein, either directly or indirectly.
Respective authors own all copyrights not held by the publisher.

Legal Notice:
This book is copyright protected. This is only for personal use. You cannot amend, distribute, sell, use, quote or paraphrase any part or the content within this book without the consent of the author or copyright owner. Legal action will be pursued if this is breached.

Disclaimer Notice:
Please note the information contained within this document is for educational and entertainment purposes only. Every attempt has been made to provide accurate, up to date and reliable complete information. No warranties of any kind are expressed or implied.

William Miyagi

Readers acknowledge that the author is not engaging in the rendering of legal, financial, medical or professional advice.

By reading this document, the reader agrees that under no circumstances are we responsible for any losses, direct or indirect, which are incurred as a result of the use of information contained within this document, including, but not limited to, — errors, omissions, or inaccuracies.

Table of Contents

INTRODUCTION 7

CHAPTER 1: ALL ABOUT ZEN 11

CHAPTER 2: THE HISTORY OF ZEN BUDDHISM 15

CHAPTER 3: BASICS OF ZEN BUDDHISM 55

CHAPTER 4: ZEN CONCEPTS 59

CHAPTER 5: HOW MEDITATION FITS IN 67

CHAPTER 6: MINDFULNESS 83

CONCLUSION 89

William Miyagi

Introduction

There's a lot to be said these days for finding anything that gives you the feeling of peace and tranquility, but you may have to thank someone from generations before you for the actual discovery. As you read through this book, you will learn how Zen was discovered and what it encompasses. You are new to this process, so I have written it in a way that doesn't mystify the subject, but that puts it in straightforward terms that anyone can understand. Why? Well, I have seen too much suffering in the world. Every day, we see so many people even in our everyday lives who are unhappy or who have troubles. The idea of introducing Zen into the lives of people who want to embrace this way of life is so that the troubles of the world are a little less.

That's a fairly positive ambition, and my life is about positivity. In fact, since taking the road to Zen, the happiness and balance that I have in my life is extraordinary. Who better then to explain that process to newcomers than someone who has incorporated that notion of inner peace into their lives? I started with very humble beginnings and graduated to a stage where I can now use Zen to give me answers to everyday problems. You see, all of the answers lie within us but sometimes the mind is too busy to see them. By incorporating Zen into your life, you are allowing your mind a certain amount of clarity but you are also adding other elements to your life which are rich sources of energy, justice and which have problem solving capacities.

Before Zen practice, I was every bit as confused as people searching for something better are. In fact, my search took me into all kinds of practices to try and find out if there was a way that was better for me than the way I was living. I'm not as humble nor as enlightened as Buddha, but he went a lot further than I did. I seek answers to personal problems. He sought answers to the problems of mankind. In fact, he was so successful at it that the Zen that you are going to learn about from reading this book, was founded many years ago by someone who cared so much about human suffering that he decided to meditate until he found the answers – and he did find the answers.

In simple terms, so that beginners can understand, this book shows you what he found and tells you how you can incorporate his teachings into your life. Does that mean you have to become a

Buddhist? Does it mean you have to wear saffron robes? Of course not. You are who you are. All Zen does is make the person that you are more aware and much happier than you think is possible.

William Miyagi

Chapter 1
All about Zen

"Holding on to anger is like grasping a hot coal with the intent of throwing it at someone else; you are the one who gets burned." ~ Gautama Buddha

At the beginning of each chapter, I am going to use a quotation from Gautama Buddha because this man was a very special man in the history of Zen. His name was Siddhartha Gautama, later known as Buddha, and what this man did was take himself away from the world into the world of meditation to find an answer to human suffering. He was convinced that the answer would come to him and he was right. Even now, we still use the philosophy that he founded as far back as the third century because it has been proven to work. What he discovered was that suffering is a result of the way that people think and Zen comes from using meditation and breathing techniques to improve awareness and thus put an end to problems. A state of Zen is a state of enlightenment or happiness and it is possible for people to achieve this through Zen Buddhism.

You may have seen Buddha statues and wondered if they are used as an icon that people worship. Actually, they are not. Buddha inspires rather than being any kind of God. Often these statues remind Buddhists of the roots of the fundamental way that they think. Christian people are taught not to be worship false idols, so I thought that getting that bit out of the way was important for a Christian audience because having a Buddha stature in your peaceful space doesn't mean anything but a reminder of our roots, and the possibilities that were originally found out when Siddhartha Gautama went on the voyage of his life, in India, a long time ago. That voyage was to change the way that he thought forever and to influence the way that people who follow Zen study think today. It was a voyage where no footsteps were needed. The voyage was one of looking inside of himself for clarity and he found it. Now you can, even if not to the same extent, and it will enrich your life and make it a happier and more fulfilled place to be.

I love the quotation made at the top of this chapter because it's so true. Okay, it doesn't have to be hot coals, but you can think of the hot coals as being translated into negativity. Think of them as anger. If you hold onto anger, what happens is that it isn't the object of your anger that feels bad long term. It's you. Anger and all the negative traits in life such as jealousy and greed eat away at who you are and you can never find enlightenment or a state of Zen while you keep hold of negative and hateful thoughts.

As you go through this book and practice the exercises shown in it, you will find your way forward in a much better way. Even though the world is a very busy place, there are still ways that you can incorporate Zen into your life and it will change who you are and make you a much more compassionate person. Compassion and empathy are central to Zen but they may not seem like the natural path to take until you start to see what happens when you do. Siddhartha Gautama found the path to enlightenment is within every human being, but that people need to follow a certain path to find it.

There are the Four Noble Truths, which are explained in a future chapter, the Eight Fold Path and the eventual aim to seek Nirvana or a state of enlightenment. Those who do are indeed fortunate to have found their way. With so many outside distractions these days, it's a wonder we can get beyond all the material things that life offers. We are told every day on our TV sets that all of these possessions hold the secret to our happiness and in truth, this kind of happiness is very shallow.

To attain a more permanent state of happiness, you need to look beyond all of the trimmings and go back to basics because it is here that the answers lie. Your peace, your happiness and wellbeing are all built in to who you are. However, the human way is to create societies that have their own rules. They have their own standards so that we are indoctrinated into believing in what's right and wrong, acceptable and non-acceptable and our minds have forgotten all about the basics that we were all born with.

Can enlightenment work for you? Yes it can, but the path there is a very definite one and thanks to the original Buddha, Gautama Buddha, he's done the work for you. He made the discovery and millions of people worldwide are only just learning that Zen still works and that it beats hands down anything commercial or material that life offers. You don't get this kind of peace from a temporary vacation or the purchase of the latest car. You get it from understanding what's inside you and how to use it to improve the way that you look at life. When you do, you will never see life in the same way again and that's pretty amazing. Not convinced yet? You will be. This book shows you how.

Chapter 2
The History of Zen Buddhism

Zen is the Japanese translation of the Sanskrit word for *dhyana*, which in turn means 'meditation'. It is a school of Buddhism which made a considerable effect on Japan, Europe and North America, the latter two locations particularly in the last 150 years. The Zen school of Buddhism originated in China during the 6th century CE, known as the Chan school of Mahayaa Buddhism and then transported to Japan during the 12th century; it was here that this particular branch evolved into a distinctive, original personality. Bodhidharma, the Indian monk, is said to have transported the philosophies from India to China. The fundamental character of his instructions is that an individual doesn't need to learn from holy writings, worship gods or even perform complicated sacred rites in order to attain enlightenment. Instead, you need to escape from the limits of conformist thought via mediation and encounter the world as it really is in the present.

Zen maintains that this belief is the exact way that the Buddha personally was able to attain enlightenment. It teaches that we all have the ability to achieve enlightenment ourselves since every one of us has an intrinsic Buddha nature; as such, we are already enlightened but our capacity has been obscured through unawareness. Several Zen customs say that this unawareness is suddenly overcome via an abrupt development – known as *satori* – whilst performing mediation where the true actuality, as well as our personal knowledge of it, is exposed. There are a number of different Zen sects, the two biggest of which are Rinzai and Soto, have developed various customs and practices in order to attain enlightenment, one of which is known as *zazen* (which then translates as 'just sitting' mediation). The fundamental philosophy of Zen is very simple, but despite this straightforwardness, instruction in Zen can be quite demanding and needs a master to direct you on your path. Zen was extremely common with samurai warriors throughout Japanese history due to its concentration on discipline and strength of mind. In addition to warrior training, it aids in different types of art including painting, gardening, archery and calligraphy. In the early 20th century, Zen was transported to Europe and North

America, and has been combined into all kinds of sports, activities and hobbies.

Influences

There were numerous elements which led to the expansion of Chan. It was believed that the Buddha practiced this type of early Buddhism himself. Huike was the second great patriarch and practiced self-discipline and dwelled in the depths of the woodlands set from the major cities. He said that it was essential to go back to the basic principles taught by Buddha – mediation and simplicity. When Chan was eventually transported to the cities and then linked with the government and administration of those areas, it carried on distinguishing itself as a sect that remained true to the principles of Buddhism.

Even though there was a great deal of importance in the early traditions and beliefs of Buddhism, it wasn't until the much later Mahayana scriptures were created that attracted to the Chan monks and intellectuals. Of specific attentiveness to the Chan school were the Perfection of Wisdom Sutras, the Garland Sutras, the Vimalakirti Sutra and the Lankavatara Sutra.

Out of numerous Buddhist thinkers, the beliefs of the Indian monk and intellectual thinker, Nagarjuna (from the 2nd to 3rd centuries) held great interest to many Chan believers due to his methodical break down of all Buddhist ethics. A number of early Buddhists sought a perception of meaninglessness through focused meditation; Nagarjuna move toward it through rational examination. By using rationality to illustrate the restrictions of any definitive elucidation for life and nothingness, of or enlightenment. If something does not have an eternal structure therefore there is no eternal truth. As such, Chan masters would use awareness and systematic methods to illustrate the confines of rational thought.

Out of the Indian branches of Buddhist philosophy that had a deep impact on the evolution of Chan were the Madhyamika and Yogacara sects. Nagarjuna is held to be the forefather of the Madhyamika (also known as the Middle Way) school by various scholars. The Middle Way School claimed that items don't possess an intrinsic character, and that realism is beyond all characteristics. There is no element to definitive enlightenment and that naught subsists autonomously of anything else. A number of intellects believe that the Middle Way School was a form of non-duality where all counterparts are obliterated. Jizang, a Chinese philosopher belonging to the Middle Way School, claimed that all things are hollow but at the same time that everything is one.

Yogacara is regularly regarded as the mind only school; as the designation suggests, some people of this belief considered that only what is in the mind truly exists. In other words, the intellect is the conjectural source of miracles. The principal supporter to the Mind Only School was Asanga, who viewed this in a very dissimilar way. He pronounced stages of judgement that would ultimately head to an encounter beyond all merits, inexplicable by the mind, subsequently leads to a revisit to the real world felt minus the illusion. Despite these dissimilarities, reflective methods and exercises geared toward accomplishing the experience of definitive truth were crucial to the Mind Only School.

It is from these theoretical thoughts that the Chan School of Buddhism would produce its own opinions regarding the Buddha nature and emptiness. Just like Candrakirti, numerous Chan intellects encouraged the breaking down of all conventional beliefs. A number of Chan believers support Jizang's views on the belief that everything is essentially empty but still one; whereas a number of Chan supporters view the breaking down of distinctions would head to the practice of viewing the real world minus the altering veil of illusion. Lastly, just as in the Yogacara School, meditative masters from the Chan school created methods to fully understand the character of consciousness. However, with Chan, the notion was to boost the intellect far beyond rationality and classes of knowledge into a condition that surpassed both rationality and experience.

Whilst various schools of Buddhist thought had a deep impact on China, outside religions would contribute. The Chinese religion of Taoism also would shape its development. The earliest written reference to Buddhism in China was from the official royal records of the Emperor Ming Di (58 – 75 CE) which recounts the experiences from a Chinese noblewoman who merged Buddhist and Taoist practices. There is another text dating from the second century CE which tells of a Taoist specialist who merged Buddhist customs to his rites in honor of the emperor. From this time came a legend which has survived into modern times with a few modifications; it tells that the Buddha was, in fact, the Taoist founder Laozi (also known as Lao Tzu) who had journeyed west from China. Another more popular version was that Laozi had travelled to India and had been the Buddha's teacher.

There are a number of similar practices in both Buddhism and Taoism, breathing exercises and concentration techniques being two of these. One Buddhist scholar travelled from Parthia to China in 148 CE and was given a local name of An Shih-kao who is famous for translation Buddhist works on these types of techniques into Chinese. There was numerous other Buddhist writings translated into Chinese during the second and third centuries concentrating on this theme.

As there were such similarities between Taoism and Buddhism, early Buddhist writings translated into Chinese incorporated many terms from Taoism. As a result, there were times when some conceptions and beliefs were often misunderstood but it did help the Chinese people find it easier to understand.

One further development in the relationship between Buddhism and Taoism started in the early fourth century when a big proportion of the Chinese nobility escaped the northern encroachment from an invasion. As they had lost their administrative powers in the northern territory, this class started to experience much free time. As a result, many took a great interest in Taoism and others ventured over to Buddhism. One particular aspect that they enjoyed was the thought that everything originates from non-being yet is still one, and overlooking all discrepancies and exploring collective accord and unison with everything.

Buddhism and Taoism, along with a new school of thought which became known as Confucianism, would help in shaping each other in numerous ways throughout the next several centuries which led to the well-known phrase – *sanjiao heyi* – which translates as *"the three teachings are united into one"*.

William Miyagi

Founders

The original founder of Chan Buddhism is Bodhidharma (known in Chinese as Damo and Daruma in Japanese) and, if we take Chan's records, is the 28th patriarch of Indian Buddhism. Late martial arts customs state that Bodhidharma stayed in the Shaolin Monastery for nine years, establishing the art of Shaolin gongfu. Bodhidharma is considered more of a legendary figure in culture but the fictional history surrounding him allows us to gain a deeper insight into how the Chan School originated and evolved in its early years.

Despite this, there is an incredible amount of interest into learning more about Bodhidharma as a historical person on his own. Certainly, there is proof to show that there was a Buddhist monk going by the name of Bodhidharma in China during the early sixth century CE, but there are no historical official records or writings to link this figure to the Chan School or even to any martial arts schools. Looking at the limited amount of evidence surrounding Bodhidharma and the beginnings of the Chan School, we can see no actual relationship at this time.

The earliest written records from China which mention Bodhidharma are from 645 CE and then revised two years later and were created by a monk named Daoxuan who also created many biographies on numerous important Buddhist monks.

However, there are many discrepancies in these writing which were compiled from a number of sources. Remarkably, the document state that Daoxuan was unware to the location of Bodhidharma's death but then later tells that he dies on the Lo River banks.

Various aspects of this famous myth are located in this biography. Daoxuan's works states that Bodhidharma was originally a Brahmin from south India who determined to journey from his home country to China in order to promote the teachings of Mahayana Buddhism. Instead of going via the Silk Route, Bodhidharma journeyed to China via boat and arrived in Nanyue. He then journeyed to Luoyang, the capital of the country at the time. However, the biography tells that his mission to convert the Chinese people to Buddhism was not primarily positive and the people began to be hostile towards him. Despite this unfriendliness, Bodhidharma was able to procure two disciples, including Huike, his heir and the second head of Chan. He dictated the Lankavatara Sutra and the renowned meditative method known commonly as wall-gazing.

As time went on, this story went on to develop new aspects and details and then incorporated the characters of other prominent monks. One prominent assertion which is important to Chan is that Bodhidharma stayed in a meditative position facing a wall for nine years, staying still for the entire time, which led to his legs falling off. An additional story tells that to avoid falling asleep during meditation, he cut off his eyelids. Whether these legends are true or not, they do stress that Bodhidharma was considered a demanding and strict master who performed the same strength of mind and dedication that his followers were expected to perform too. It is claimed that Huike cut off his arm in order to illustrate his dedication to Buddhism and his teacher.

Certain traits taken from the identities of particular Taoist gods or immortals were ascribed onto Bodhidharma. One of these traits was that he faked his own death and changed an item in so that it resembled the shape of a deceased body. When someone proclaimed that they had seen him travelling back to India, his burial place was undone and only one straw sandal was discovered.

In Japan, Bodhidharma was known commonly as Daruma and became highly popular with the Tendai Buddhist school. After it developed into an independent school from the Tendai sect, it was called the Japanese School of Bodhidharma. A particular myth from Japan states that Bodhidharma had disguised himself as a beggar and came across Prince Shotoku, a famous supporter of Japanese Buddhism. The prince wrapped the beggar in his coat and gave him food and water. Prince Shotoku inquired of the beggar later on but discovered he had died and ordered him buried. After this, the prince started to believe that the beggar was something more than just a beggar; his grave was re-opened and they discovered just the coat inside.

The Daruma toy can be found in many homes across Japan. It reminds you of one of the boppy toys; it features a round curved base and is legless, so it cannot fall over at all. The Daruma doll is believed to represent good luck, security and success. There are numerous paintings of Daruma from all periods of Japanese history showing him in well-known light – projecting eyes without eyelids, an unkempt beard, and no hair with a ferocious look upon his face.

Just with Bodhidharma, we still don't know much about the historical individual known as Huineng. Our main source of knowledge of him comes from Henhui, who is credited with the contention that he was the primary heir of Hongren, the fifth patriarch of Chan, but even with this claim he wasn't able to deliver any historical information for Huineng's epigraph. What we do know comes to a limited amount of facts: that he is recorded as one of several important pupils of Hongren and when he died, his family home in southern China was given to the *sangha* to be transformed into a temple.

Just as with Bodhidharma, it is the myth surrounding Huineng which is far more significant to Chan customs. The difference between the two individuals is that Bodhidharma's legend evolved over several hundred years yet the majority of Huineng's myth is discovered within the Platform Sutra, where his life's story is recounted and his climb to as the sixth head. Within the Platform Sutra illustrates Huineng's rank as the head as well as producing different the numerous sects which were founded before Chan into a comprehensible institution.

Numerous central notions from Chan are illustrated in the Platform Sutra's account of Huineng. A particular notion is that enlightenment can be transferred from individual to another individual immediately. The previously established written customs of Buddhism were thought to be substandard to this notion of transferring enlightenment. In addition to this notion was the thought that enlightenment could be attained by anyone, irrespective of education, teaching or social background. As a result, these beliefs were elaborated further throughout the centuries and presented them in numerous ways.

Sacred Texts

Chan is often said to be a "special transmission outside the scriptures"; this phrase is often accredited to Bodhidharma when in fact it originated centuries later. Many scholars have expressed the theory that it means language is not necessary in Chan, whereas other scholars argue that it refers to the Chan notion that enlightenment is able transferable directly via individual to individual.

Chan is especially recognized for its mysterious and illogical legends, but it has also expressed intellectual examinations of various writings, and that the Buddhist standard is just as important to Chan like to the other Buddhist schools. Another aspect which connects Chan to other Buddhist sects is that it also features general ritual rites which featured sacred texts, for example, vocalizing writings in ceremonies. It is the Platform Sutra which is key to the custom and the story inside the sutra founds the myth of Huineng.

Chan Buddhism has also been influenced through several other sutras. These include the Diamond Sutra and the Heart Sutra. The former is key for Huineng as he is said to have experience an understanding when he first heard it spoken, resulting in him venturing to the north to explore Buddhism.

The Heart Sutra was incredibly widespread with numerous Buddhist sects and is still used in Chan monasteries today.

The Heart Sutra and the Diamond Sutra feature in the script Prajnaparamita, also known as the Perfect of Wisdom Sutra. This central subject is that wisdom is beyond words and that it is essentially empty as that it does not possess a separate inherent nature.

The next sutras which had a deep impact on Chan were the Garland Sutra and the Huayen School. This is because they swayed Chan thinkers with their beliefs on the accord and union of everything. Various comparisons are illustrated in these sutras. One such is the following: a pearl necklace was strung over the Indian god Indra's palace, each pearl linked with the others, all mirroring the others to the degree that you only needed to look at one to see them all. Another comparison, most likely from the Lankavatara Sutra, uses ocean waves to explain. In this, the waves of the ocean are basically a movement of the ocean – all waves essentially blends into the next.

The unqualified supporter of Buddhism known as Vimalakirti was highly regarded to many of the other unqualified people to follow Chan. Indeed, the Vimalakirti Sutra is the one sutra which has been translated in Chinese far more than the rest. A particular section of this sutra gives a detailed explanation for mediating than purely sitting silently beneath a tree in the woods. It tells how to promote a reflective frame of mind whilst dealing with day to day life and it is this notion which became a prominent part of Chan customs. An additional section tells how a gathering of bodhisattvas (Buddhas in training) enquired of Vimalakirti what it signifies to join the dharma of non-dualism. It was said he replied that it meant to be silent. As such, this has been referred to as the 'thunderous silence of Vimalakirti'.

The Lankavatara Sutra was another significant sutra in Chan tradition. It is the story of when the Buddha journeyed to the island of Lanka (modern day Sri Lanka). The Chan myth states that Bodhidharma imparted the wisdom in the Lankavatara Sutra to Huike; this is why the Chan school is occasionally referred to as the Lankavatara School. In the following centuries, some of the notions found in this sutra would be used in the Yogacara School.

There were various questions presented to the reader within the Lankavatara Sutra, one being how an individual can acquire karma and where is it kept? The comeback was that there are eight states of consciousness, with the last state referred to as the storehouse consciousness (also known as alaya vijnana), where all the karma from former experiences are accumulated. At times this karma can evoke long memories and kindle the method that allows the reincarnation of conscious creatures. If an individual can grasp the emptiness of everything at this last 'warehouse' state, and then the cycle of rebirth can be ceased. This notion of a termination of reincarnation and the ultimate truth of intellect was particularly attractive to the Chan scholars. But this enlightenment was not the comprehension of a frame of mind outside general reality.

The comprehension of the mind's true character may have originated from the Chan custom of gongan, also known as an encounter dialogue (in Japan it is called koan). Two of the most renowned followers of this particular method were Shitou Xiqian (710 – 790 CE) and Mazu Daoyi (709 – 788 CE) and are known as the founders of the Linji and Caodong branches of the Chan school (known as Rinazi and Soto in Japanese). The most famous out of all masters of this practice was Linji Yixuan, who died in 867 CE, who coined the saying "If you meet the Buddha, kill him!" which is still a popular phrase even today in Chan schools.

However, with this it is important to stress the fact there are no texts from this period which state that either Shitou or Mazu used the encounter practice. The earliest mention of this practice is found within the Anthology of the Patriarchal Hall, dating back to 952 CE. This text is additionally an example of the beginnings of the 'transmission of the lamp' writings; this is essentially a list of all the heads of the Chan tradition which originated in India right up to the date of its compilation. Many of these compilations gives us vital information on the biographies of highly regarded monks and their encounter dialogues which would be arranged in various distinct compendiums which would feature writings from additional individuals.

Dedicated gongan practices are typically confined into Chan monasteries, numerous texts focusing on these practices have been published over the years, making them accessible to inexperienced students. As such, their mysterious character is often regarded as a distinctive to the Chan School.

Human Nature and the Reason for Existence

The purpose of existence and understanding human nature has been focused on in Zen and the way to do this through the notion of the Buddha-nature. The dialogue regarding the Buddha-nature evolved through the Buddhist customs due to an apparent inconsistency concerning the dogma of no-self (also known as anatman) and the capability of someone to achieve enlightenment. We can clearly see in the earliest writings that claim that the secret to enlightenment is the understanding that there isn't a distinct perpetual self, that complete control over oneself was described by the Buddha. Not only this, but apprehensions arose over the dogma regarding that no-self was seen as destructive as it appeared to a few that the closure of self would only bring one to extinction.

William Miyagi

The topic of self-nature was argued between Yogacara and Madhyamika intellects and was expressed within Mahayana texts. Breaking the topic down into an extremely basic argument, on one hand scholars were claiming that everyone was an fundamental part of Buddha-nature, on another hand scholars were suggesting that there is not this type of physical principle, other scholars claiming that it does and doesn't exist, and additional scholars suggesting that the misconception of division between the self and Buddha-nature continued merely up to the point when an individual achieved enlightenment.

These arguments between the various intellectual thinkers gave rise to the notion that there existed two realisms, the first being known as the absolute and the other as the relative. The absolute was authentic, whereas the relative was tainted, and in order to come to know the absolute first you have to push away the other. However, there are those who state that nothing can be achieved in actuality, since achievement is a disillusion of its own between absolute and relative; as a result, everything which is present possesses Buddha-nature. In addition to this, there are intellects which claim that both realisms are equally pure, the absolute being the manifestation of pure wisdom whereas the relative being the manifestation of pure compassion.

Zen

There is not a definitive reply to this argument in Chan (or Zen). Within the Huineng account, Shenxiu backs the notion of purity of the absolute, the depiction of cleaning the mirror of oneself of contaminations to expose a pure mind. Huineng's reply stated that the mirror and the mind simply don't exist and nothing can be achieved as one is already there.

Various Zen schools promote a quiet meditative tradition known as zazen whereas other schools don't, or not on purpose. The custom of zazen is perceived for many as a method to purify the mind of obstacles so that one can expose their potential Buddha-nature. On the other hand, other practitioners see it as a representation of the nothingness of oneself yet is still a way to understand Buddha-nature.

The reason for existence in the Zen traditions is to basically enjoy a conventional life but still being aware of one's responsibilities. This is particularly illustrated in the fact that Huineng was said to have been tasked with chopping firewood and winnowing rice upon coming to the monastery yet still being referred to as the one student which had the utmost comprehension of the master's wisdoms. There are a number of phrases within Zen that back this story up.

For the majority of us, the things we do are typically done on a day to day basis without too much thought put into it. Within Zen thought, this absence of thought proves the separation between the person and the rest of the world. Instead of experiencing the current moment, we are often looking forward to know what we need or should be done, or behind us to remember what has happened. When we pay attention to what we are doing in the exact moment, even in the day to day tasks which have to be done, it shows that we are, in fact, aware of what is going on around us and gives us the chance to understand the Buddha-nature within ourselves and others.

Another thing we need to realize is that one particular aspect of Zen is not really connected with theories of human nature, yet still conveys an unspoken comprehension of it is the custom of shock treatment. Within the history of Zen teaching there are numerous tales of bullying masters who beat their students and even go as far as mutilating them. This is also reflected in the various exercises in Zen monasteries, which include consistent whacks with the keisaku, also known in English as 'the encouragement stick'. It is believed that these assaults will shock the receiver into enlightenment and the tales often claim that this is the result of such beatings.

The Zen texts don't actually claim that human nature is wicked but the commonality of these tales and the exercise of the encouragement sticks assaulting someone does imply a conjecture regarding human nature. We do see an insinuation within these tales that there is something deep inside an individual incredibly obstinate and disobedient that the only way it can be driven out is through a physical attack.

Suffering and the Issue with Evil

When looking at the overall picture, we see that the Zen's view in regards to suffering and the issues with evil is pretty much the same as in Mahayana Buddhism. We can understand more fully the Zen viewpoint of these difficulties within the "On Faith in Mind", also known as the Xinxin Ming, a particular style of poetry which is generally identified to Sengsan, the third head of the Zen school.

The actual history of Sengsan is severely limited but the stories surrounding him say that when he came before Huike and declared that he was suffering with an atrocious disease (numerous texts state it was leprosy), he requested that Huike pardon his sins in order to be cured. Huike told him to bring forth his sin in order to be pardoned to which Sengsan responded that he couldn't reach his sin to do this. Huike told him that he he therefore pardoneded him. This tale is a renowned koan with Zen history.

Numerous theories have arisen regarding when Xinxin Ming was created and who the author was, but academics do agree it was created several centuries after Sengsan died. There is a very apparent Taoist effect on the transcript; not only do we see the distinctive philosophies expressed but also in the Taoist and Confucian sayings used, for example, wu-wei.

The Xinxin Ming claims that all the sorrow and discontent in the world originates with dualism concepts. The opening to the text states *"The Great Way is not difficult for those who have no preferences"*; this inclination can be perceived as an approach incredibly hard to achieve.

However, this is not essential a suggestion to attain this state of mind; it is essentially a description of reality. Just as with Nagarjuna, the writer who created the Xinxin Ming suggests that everything is not real or real, that it's not empty and is empty. If you look at things with an 'or' and 'either' way then you are being tricked by illusion.

Using an examination quite alike to the Four Noble Truths, that suggests all suffering originates from desire, the Xinxin Ming claims that the development of generating differences and preferences results in human suffering. Discerning between various distinctions results in beliefs of 'right' and 'truth' which in itself is confusing as there is no accord between the two. In actuality, there are delusions resulting from dualism.

The Xinxin Ming claims that the answer to this is to recognize that everything is one and when you are able to recognize this, then you will be in accord with the rest of the world. Upon his meeting with Huike, Sengsan understood this. His pain and misery from his affliction wasn't derived from an evil act that he had performed previously and that it couldn't, or even required, to be eliminated from his person through pardoning.

The story tells that Sengsan did, in fact, recover from his affliction and ultimately achieved physical freedom from it. There are a number of thoughts of this, one of which saw it as being a general human desire for a happy ending or even as a method to contradict the possible destructive explanations of Xinxin Ming. It allows the reader to understand that at a very basic level, everything is one with each other.

Sacred Space in Zen Buddhism

There are a number of different types of sacred spaces within Chan and Zen schools of thought. Sacred spaces are recognized as being sanctified areas via a belief of the manifestation of the sacred, spaces which are decreed sacred through ceremonies, and a general sense of a perception of the awareness of the sacred. We don't just see this notion of sacred spaces in just Zen or Chan, but the belief of a sacred space as an embodiment of sacredness is typically identified with them.

The concept of sacred space originates from Shinto and most probably from the native customs before the establishment of Shinto itself. It was believed that any area in which a deity appears is considered to be a sacred space. Because of this, it is commonly thought that all Japanese temples were erected on the sites where gods (also known as *kami*) had shown themselves to human beings. We also see this same belief in ancient Chinese, where certain areas were perceived to be sacred when believed to be occupied by a supernatural presence, and many folktales mirror this notion.

In each of these concepts, the god or paranormal creature as well as the space it appeared were believed to be the same; as such, many natural aspects (such as trees, rivers etc) were thought to be the physical manifestations of these gods. Numerous Chan and Zen temples were erected on sites which had been considered a sacred space long before.

The other type of sacred space is a progression of the former type; it is the area which becomes sacred due to a rite. As an example, the location where either a god, a divine manifestation or even a paranormal being had materialized may possibly turn out to be a pilgrimage spot, or the surrounding area where a sacred occurrence may well be arranged as a mandala; guests may tread in an ordered outline that represented the mandala's form.

When applied all together, we can clearly see that all ceremonial actions within Buddhism could be regarded as an evocation of the sacred, welcoming a sacred manifestation or producing a sacred space. If we look at the latter type of sacred space then we can see that it transforms a precise and explicit familiarity of the sacred as something far more nonrepresentational, and then it makes a native custom a universal concept.

Now let us take a look at the notions surrounding the last kind of sacred space. Both Zen and Chan produced their own generalized sacred spaces which centered on their own significant occurrences within their customs. As an example, the wall that Bodhidharma was claimed to have looked at during meditation became a sacred space within Zen.

This third notion of sacred space originates in Indian Buddhism and not exclusive to Chan or Chan, but it has now been identified with this custom especially. Since it is taught that everything has a Buddha-nature, everything you do, regardless of how boring or exciting it is, can become a representation and express sacredness. As a result then, every space is really a sacred space, and includes the space within you. You may say that this is a

39

perpetual type of sacred space and that this sacredness of all space is exposed upon understanding that every single thing in the universe has a Buddha-nature.

Since the third notion of sacred space has evolved from a specific manifestation of the celestial, it becomes something far more intangible and collective. Powerful and insightful happenstances with the native gods allowed the development of a permeating awareness of serenity and harmonious accord with all life. As this is happening, the possible influence of native gods and supernatural beings to sway human life is likewise counterbalanced through this procedure of generalization.

When Chan and Zen are truly observed, these three different kinds of sacred space don't really substitute each other. When people visit Chan or Zen temples, they discover that all three notions of sacred space are commemorated there. This includes the monuments erected to native paranormal beings and creatures, holy sites or mandalas to navigate and halls where monks can meditate and study the sacred.

Rites and Ceremonies

As with the majority of Buddhist monks across the world, Chan and Zen monks will spend a great deal of time overseeing the rites for the help of the untrained members. There are numerous occasions when they do this during the Buddhist ceremonial calendar, particularly in Japan and especially in the annual celebration of the Ghost Festival. This is where the souls of the deceased come back to call in on the living. Zen monks will oversee these ceremonial rites for people, especially funerary rituals and other rites concerning the deceased.

The organization of contemporary Buddhist funerary rituals in Japan originated from the funerary rites for the Chan high priests that materialized in 11th century CE China. Although the funerary customs for general Chan monks were developed in order to safeguard their incarnation into the Pure Land, the customs for the high priests within the Chan school developed from various Confucian customs surrounding the funerary rites for the elite social classes, especially those that center around the burial practices for one's mother and father. A particular Chan aspect concerning the higher priests was that they would be put into a rounded casket in the position of seating meditation.

Towards the end of the 13th century in Japan, this funerary organization had been expanded and all Zen Buddhist believers were buried in this manner. Images of the dead were portrayed; they were proclaimed as a Buddhist monk and, in addition to all of this, were presented a Buddhist name and certificate which their new Buddhist name was featured on at the end of this scroll.

As a result, the deceased was transformed into an enlightened Zen monk.

Aspects of this particular ceremonial organization had been included in every Zen funeral by the latter part of the 15th century in Japan. This wasn't just limited to the socially elite, but included all other social classes and there is evidence to support this notion for the lower classes as well. The dead were proclaimed and clothed as Zen monks, even going as far as to shave their heads. Cremation was the general method of disposing the body and a ceremony similar to what may happen during a koan encounter was performed whilst the body was being cremated. This ceremony was a representation of how the deceased could attain enlightenment even after they had died.

The inauguration of someone becoming a Zen monk once dead was a standard practice but it was also associated with rituals that allowed many Buddhist supporters to become monks whilst living, all agreeing to follow the principles which all monks had to abide by. Those participating in these rituals vowed not to lie, kill, steal and other types of wicked behavior, in addition to taking bodhisattva oaths to delay their individual enlightenment until every other conscious creature had gained their own freedom from illusion. Once you had taken the oaths, you were bound to it no matter what happened in the future.

It was probable that there was a good amount of rivalry with the Pure Land Buddhism in this progression of establishing a short cut to a finer reincarnation. On one hand, the general Zen and Chan believers were given an simpler way to achieve enlightenment, but it also made things far harder for the priests when needing to create the spiritual power required to make certain that the dead could achieve enlightenment as well as those living.

In modern day Japan, the majority of funerals held are Buddhist and there is still the age-old custom of assigning a Buddhist name to the person who died. A tablet is presented to the family of the deceased with his or hers Buddhist name which is then taken home and positioned on the *butsudan* (known in English as the Buddhist altar found in the house). The family will then light incense and recite sutras. It is believed that this is a successful way of guaranteeing a better position in the hereafter, but the strength it holds is far lesser from the former ceremonial customs.

To become an ordained Buddhist monk one must undergo formal training and many will go to Buddhist colleges and universities to do this. Quite a number of people who aren't even members of the Zen school will visit the Zen monasteries to train, due to the greatly ritualized traditions. Students are required to meditate on a day to day basis, as well as particular highly focused lessons known as *sesshin*, which typically lasts for seven days and performed around six times annually. Meditation exercises can last up to 20 hours daily, not including walking meditation (known as kinhin), meetings with the temple master, all with performing the general day to day chores.

Zen monasteries belonging to the Rinzai sect will generally give a koan to those training to be a monk, and are expected to focus on this continually. When they meet with their master, they will offer potential replies towards the koan, and these replies will be either acknowledged or prohibited. The master might criticize them, ridicule them or even go as far as strike them if they do not give them the right answer. This practice is believed to ensure that they want to hold the koan even more than before. When the koan is believed to have been fully understood by the monk, then the master will present him with a different one.

For monks who want to dedicate themselves to the study of spiritual progression, there are numerous programs which offer extended training. Participants in these kinds of programs will study both Zen and general Buddhist scriptures, having to memorize extended passages and create regular essays and poetry, writing both using the calligraphy brush.

The majority of the monks in training do not participate in such programs in monasteries. Instead, many will stay in the monasteries to work towards being a family priest and do not always show the same amount of commitment and thoroughness as those who are studying to become a Zen scholar. Zen painting and poetry has been considered incredibly beautiful and brilliant but are not typically included in most Zen monastery's lessons.

Symbolism

There are many symbols from Zen Buddhism that can be found in various other schools but there are several which are exclusive to Zen and Chan). The symbol for Zen is the *enso*, which appears to be a circle created from one stroke of the brush and can be small or big. It doesn't matter if the circle is perfect or imperfect and even though it is one of the simplest symbols to create, a limited number of painters have been recognized for their brilliant *enso*.

The *enso* can be translated in a number of different ways. It can be the representation of bareness or completeness, presence or a lack of presence. Everything can be kept inside or barred by its borders. It may be the symbol of enlightenment, of the moon (another symbol for enlightenment).

William Miyagi

Paintings are considered to be a great way of presenting the principles of Zen in a visual way. Hakuin, a Rinzai Zen Master from the 18th century was considered to be one of the great Zen painters. In addition to this, poetry was regarded as another manner in which to promote one's consciousness of Zen understanding. Ryokan, Basho and Ikkyu are just three world-renowned Zen poets who were able to use Zen descriptions, especially referring to nature and mentions actual historical Zen characters and locations in their works. We also see references to mysterious customs from Buddhism and Taoism.

In Japan, there were several notable monk poets who produced this type of poetry but were not members of any Zen schools, in particularly Saigyo and Ippen. Wang Wei from China is another notable painter and poet who was linked with Chan but he wasn't actually a Buddhist monk; indeed, he was actually a governmental official. When we look at Zen poetry in an academic light, we see more of a generalization of Buddhist inspiration instead of a Zen impact. Various artistic practices (i.e. gardening, martial arts, tea ceremonies etc) have regularly been influenced by Zen but are not unique to it.

The rock garden is the most common type of garden which is linked with Zen. Circular motifs made from little white stones are created using a wooden rake. At times, several bigger stones are placed amongst the numerous little pebbles. The symbolization behind these Zen gardens is simplicity, serenity, meticulousness and uniformity order. The motifs are meant to be recreated on a daily basis and this is considered to be a means of meditation. The most renowned Zen rock garden is located at Ryoanji in Kyoto, Japan.

A number of academics have put forward the theory that the notion of the rock garden being a character for Zen is quite a current hypothesis and may have been a creation of post-Meiji Japanese patriotism. Other scholars have claimed that whilst the Zen rock garden may not have originated in the actual Zen tradition, it is still able to motivate people in the custom.

We can see quite a different way showing Zen symbolization when we look at Zen temple architecture, especially in Japan. The basic outline is founded on ancient Chinese temple architecture that was, in actuality, was founded on a amalgamation of Buddhist architecture from India and Chinese design standards.

The entrance to Zen temples are known as the Mountain Gate and it is the symbol for journeying over the border from earthly desires and theoretical intellect into nothingness. From the central position is the Buddha Hall, which is created for the monks to worship the Buddha and the bodhisattvas (buddhas in training). Prior to coming into the Buddha Hall, it is imperative to get rid of all contaminations and thoroughly wash yourself. Not far from the Mountain Gate are two little rooms designed for this. In all these rooms, particularly in the Buddha Hall, you must remain silent.

Head further down past the Buddha Hall and you will discover the Monk's Hall. This is the location were monks will come to meditate. Facing the Buddha Hall is the kitchen. Combining the Monk's Hall and the kitchen comes to symbolize feeding the mind and the body. Last but not least, is the Dharma Hall; this is the location where the monks come together to listen to talks and orations. Of course, Zen monasteries will feature numerous other buildings in the complex.

A similarity is occasionally made between the organization of the Zen monastery complex and specific locations of the human body or that of the Buddha's body. Mountain Gate, as the entrance of the monastery complex, is referred to as the groin; the Buddha Hall is a representation of the heart; and the Dharma Hall symbolizes the head. The right leg is represented by the bathhouse, the toilet being the left leg. The kitchen is seen to symbolize the right arm, the left arm is represented by the left arm. When you step into the monastery complex it symbolizes the belief that you are stepping into the Buddha's body, or that you are becoming the Buddha himself.

Another symbolization in Zen and Chan schools is that of the monks' robes. Every school and sect in Buddhism across the world has their own unique style of robes, which will differ in coloring and designs. However, it should be stressed that this is not just unique to Zen. One of Zen's most identifiable robe is that of the purple robe, the color symbolizing when the color was a gifted to esteemed monastery masters. Even today, the saying "received the purple robe" is a phrase used to refer to someone becoming the leader of a Zen temple.

In history, the earliest purple robes were given by the Chinese Empress Wu to a assemblage of monks, as well as her lover, and eventually the tradition of giving purple robes were transported to Japan. When the leader of a Zen monastery was given a purple robe, it gave the temple or monastery an increased sense of prestige as well as an increase of donations from the public. However, there were times when the purple robes were centered on scandals in China and Japan. At these times, the prominent purple robes were brought by rich citizens along with inauguration scrolls. The founder of the Soto Zen school in Japan, known as Dogen, was presented with the purple robes numerous times but kept declining them until ultimately he accepted them but refused to wear them because he wanted to stay away from political relationships.

William Miyagi

Principles of Moral Thought and Action

Even before Buddhism was introduced into either China or Japan, the citizens in these countries had already had firm concepts of morality and Buddhism itself had already been well established long before the Chan and Zen schools emerged onto the scene. As such, the Zen school didn't really require a distinctive moral code. Just as with all other Buddhist followers, the monks from the Zen sect would abide by the principles of Buddhism and all monasteries and temples had exacting guidelines and conventions that they expected to be followed.

These principles have been adapted and modified to some extent throughout the various Buddhist schools, as well as the offshoot Zen schools such as Rinazi and Soto. Monks have to agree to follow the rules which included not killing, not engaging in stealing, not to gossip, not to put the blame onto someone else, not to take drugs and not to perform in sexual activities, to name just a few. There are an additional 200 rules within the Dharmagupta Vinaya that Chan monks agree to abide by. Zen monks swear to uphold the bodhisattva oath in which they delay their own enlightenment until everyone else has attained their own enlightenment. An important element within Zen is that one must have compassion and show it.

As Buddhism was transported into Europe, the Americas and the rest of the world, some Zen monasteries and scholars have attempted to modify the principles somewhat for this new audience. Let's look at the Zen monk, Thich Nhat Hanh (born in 1926), as an example. Thich Nhat Hanh was born in Vietnam and developed a large audience in the western world and has produced a collection of 14 principles for the contemporary Buddhist. Some of these include not to force anyone (including children) to follow your beliefs; not to ignore the suffering of others; and do not use Buddhism to gain wealth or for political means.

Thich Nhat Hanh is one of several modern supporters of Engaged Buddhism; this is an effort which focuses on compassionate activities instead of isolating oneself in a monastery or temple. Although performing helpful acts is not a requirement or even a principle in Buddhism, Zen, as with the other Buddhist sects, have constantly performed good acts amongst the community. A number of criticizers of persistent or preaching forms of Engaged Buddhism claim that the act of quietness and contemplation are successful ways to change the world.

In the western world, Zen has become known as the sect who offers flexibility and a lack of boundaries, even though training in Zen requires an exacting and rigid form of chastisement. There are a number of scholars who believe that the breaking down trait of Zen's viewpoints gives it a rather dishonorable atmosphere, or that Zen doesn't even separate between good and bad. It could be that this viewpoint came about from the koans being used as historical facts when, in fact, when they were shown performing ferocious acts in order to be shocking to the viewer and not really the actual way Zen monks and nuns really lived. On the other hand, there are other scholars who suggest that the individuals who view the world clearly – which were one of the main objectives in Zen – will lead to someone unsurprisingly acting ethically. The lack of existential fact doesn't disaffirm morals; ethical conduct comes from the exact moment that one finds oneself experiencing at that time.

Untrained Zen followers could also take on these oaths when it felt as though they had learnt enough they were allowed to take the bodhisattva oath. The majority of those who took these oaths did so with determination and dedication, but there were instances throughout history when the Zen monasteries conducted collective inauguration ceremonies in addition to selling ordination documentations. This was indeed a type of exploitation of such oaths which could be compared to the selling of indulgences in the Catholic Church in medieval Europe. Some people believed that if they took these oaths then it would pardon them from any negative actions that they had previously done.

Although when Zen funerals allowed the dead to be classed as Buddhist monks and proclaimed to have attained enlightenment it could be regarded as a type of manipulation, and it is possible they this was the original intention of this, there is no evidence that it led to bad moral behavior amongst general society. In addition to this, it didn't lead to the elimination of how people viewed the souls of the dead, or how the rites conducted in connection with the dead were performed, such as setting paper money alight and burning incense. Instead, they were practiced alongside other means to ensure that the souls of their loved ones would be comfortable in the hereafter. In China, many Taoist believers will also perform some of these rites and the Chinese rite, Pudu, is allowed to be conducted by both a Buddhist and Taoist priest.

William Miyagi

Chapter 3
Basics of Zen Buddhism

"No one saves us but ourselves. No one can and no one may. We ourselves must walk the path." ~ Gautama Buddha

I suppose that the western equivalent of the saying shown above is that every man is an island. We can all recognize and empathize with that view, as it's a common thing known to everyone. What may not be so obvious is the path that takes us there. The Four Noble Truths are not something mystical or beyond your capability. These are as follows:

Dukkha

Dukkha is the first truth. This is the truth of suffering. We all know this exists, so it becomes the first truth in the Four Noble Truths.

When you want to find out answers to an equation, you have to put together all of the elements and then use this information to derive an answer. This is what the four truths do.

Samudaya

The words may be foreign to you, but the sentiment behind them is less so. Samudaya means the cause of suffering. Thus for every suffering, there is a cause. We also know this to be true, so it's not unreasonable to include it into the equation.

Nirhodha

This means that all suffering finds an end. Think of a pain that you had. It doesn't last. There is always an end. The unhappiness you suffered in the past ended when something else replaced it. Thus this becomes one of the Four Truths.

Magga

This truth is a little more important because it constitutes the path that we take to end suffering.

Thus you can see that Zen is very organized in the way that it dissects a problem, finds the cause and ends the problem. It may seem very simplistic to someone who is accustomed to complex thought patterns, but that's one of the reasons that so many people miss what is so obvious. They make complex that which isn't. The idea of Zen is to unravel all of those preconceptions and make life simpler so that you can find the cause of suffering and put it to an end. In the western world, life is very complex. In the workplace, you may have deadlines to meet, you may find that time is a very valuable asset and that you don't have enough of it. You may experience stress and may even suffer depression as a result of having your mind overstretched all the time by the pressures of life. Zen allows you to step back, even in a busy life, and find the inner way. Believe me, I found it every bit as amusing or ironic as you may be right now. I said all the things I expect you to be saying, but when I actually grasped the idea and used it in my everyday life, it made so much sense, saved me so much time and in the process made me a much better person.

The Eight Fold Path simplified

The path that you take to reach Magga may seem a little complex but let's break it down into easy to swallow steps. The Eight Fold Path is what Buddhists call it. I want to simplify this because if I start to introduce even more difficult to remember words at this stage, you may miss the point and that's not the purpose of this book. The Eight Fold Path includes the following elements:

- ✓ Right view or right understanding – That's not hard to understand.

- ✓ Right emotions – This one's easy. Compassion and Empathy come top on the list.
- ✓ The right way to communicate – all positive stuff that you can relate to.
- ✓ The right action – this is a question of ethics and again is easy to understand.
- ✓ The right livelihood – This means working in a non-exploitive environment.
- ✓ The right attitude – This is all about the energy and attitude of your approach.
- ✓ The right mindfulness – This means being aware
- ✓ The right mindset – This means absorbing the ideas of Buddhism and your awareness of such.

Thus you can see that it's fairly straightforward. If you run a sweat shop and exploit your workers, cheat your customers and swear a lot, without noticing the effect that your actions have on others, you're not Buddhist and you are not taking the eight fold path.

Chapter 4
Zen Concepts

In this section we will take a look at some various key concepts in Zen.

Mushotoku

The idea of Mushotoku in Zen epitomizes the mind-set whereby the soul doesn't look to achieve a thing. This is the standpoint of a mind that doesn't allow itself to bond with material things and doesn't seek to gain a profit for oneself.

If you don't have this mind-set, then the zazen is not genuine. Worldly wisdom originates in Mushotoku and it goes beyond dualism and the boundaries our attitude creates. When you become one with the notion of Mushotoku then you have gained happiness and freedom in all events.

William Miyagi

This particular notion of performing acts and not expecting anything in return, offering without anticipations, can be the hardest notion for Westerners to realize as wanting something in exchange for something else is quite an everyday attitude.

Zazen, or Zen meditation, should not be conducted when you are hoping, or expecting, to gain something from it. Do not practice zazen if you want to make a profit, be gifted with a prize or even to achieve mysterious supernatural powers.

Zazen should only be conducted for zazen sake. There is no actual subject in zazen – it is the union of oneself with the universe. One must also aspire to be Mushotoku in martial arts too.

In your day to day life, it is very easy to desire something that you don't possess and it is normal to hold onto what you have. There are some individuals who continually want more than what they already have, thinking of how to acquire more of what they want and if they give something to someone, how to get something in exchange.

However, there are times when you have to achieve something more in order to live. Someone who works in finance does need to ensure that he earns a profit. But if he only concentrates on that profit then he will be deprived of a genuine zazen custom.

In Zen, Mushotoku requires that you rid yourself from all connections regarding personal profit. As a result, you release your inner self, and this is the best accomplishment that you will ever attain.

Mushotoku, as such, is the mind-set of acting with expecting or desiring an accomplishment and this method characterizes the path of the Buddha and of Zen.

Hishiryo

Hishiryo is the mind-set past contemplating and non-thinking. When practicing zazen, this is the normal behavior of the consciousness.

The way your consciousness behaves when engaging in meditation is not the way it does in your day to day life. When you practice zazen, your thoughts will come and go naturally – it is extremely customary behavior. When you allow these thoughts to materialize and then vanish normally, without probing deeper into them, then the mind experiences peacefulness on its own and this is when Hishiryo consciousness starts.

If you should continually think about things then your mind-set is not acting normally. Your imaginings and particular wants are communicating right into your brain, guiding you from your mind's uncomplicated, quiet, primary state.

When you are constantly thinking then you become more scared and grow far more fretful as you continue. When this carries on for an extended time, the mind can go crazy and impediments occur. Conflictions emerge and you find that you cannot locate the peace and serenity that you need. It stops your connection with the universe.

It is only when you cease this inner activity that you can go back to the undemanding and passive state of mind.

The concept of Hishiryo can be seen in animals; they live in the present moment and as a result, they are linked with the universe.

Zanshin

Zanshin is a notion within Zen, Budo (a form of martial arts originating in Japan), Kendo and other artistic activities such as flower arranging, ink painting (known as sumi-e) and the chado tea ceremony.

In its most basic form, Zanshin is the mind-set whereby the mind if completely aware of what is going on around them; it is when the mind stays motionless without being connected to anything and is completely present when you do anything.

The whole universe is affected by our way of thinking; this includes what we say to each other, how we act to other people and how we move.

Everything that you do in the present moment should be ethical and well balanced – this is Zanshin. All the things you do is significant in the universe, even if it is just as boring as brushing your teeth or having a conversation with someone else. You should do every little act with Zanshin in mind.

The notion of Zanshin is that you should be completely aware of what you are doing or being involved in at the time it is happening. When you eat, be completely involved in eating. When you fight, be completely involved in the fight. When you write, be completely involved in the act of writing.

When applied to the art of Budo, Zanshin is the awareness of where you are and what your enemies are doing, prepared for action and not being influenced by physical pain. It takes many years of study to achieve this mind-set. By incorporating the acts of zazen and Budo into your day to day life, you will come to understand that there are no commonplace moments.

Fudoshin

Fudoshin is known as the 'immovable mind', the notion that the mind has already dealt with every trial and has achieved a mind-set of ultimate self-control and boldness. This condition of peace is necessary when using zazen and Budo.

Fudoshin characterizes a serene mind-set of complete dedication and immovable resolve. This is the mind-set of a spirit resolute on winning and is full of bravery, stamina and willpower to overcome all obstacles in its path. As such, Fudoshin is linked with the sentiment of indestructability, and cannot be disrupted via chaos, hesitancy, distrust or even fright.

During the feudal period in Japanese history, the concept of Fudoshin was offered within the Samurai's indisputable presentation of courage and determination to confront hurdles, threats, pain and death without fear.

From a westerner's mind-set, the notion of any warrior lacking wrath, instead being a calm peaceful warrior, is sometimes met with confusion. It can be incredibly hard to merge the notion of ferocity with a peaceful mind-set, but it is this conception that made the Samurai warriors what they were and was the heart of martial arts themselves.

Within day to day life, Fudoshin is the barrier, the shield if you will, between us and the four mental illnesses; anger, doubt, fear and surprise. Through continual custom of zazen, one can learn to empty one's mind and develop a Fudoshin mind-set.

Mushin

Mushin is the heart of Zen and Budo and can simply be translated as the "mind without mind", or generally referred to as "the state of no-mindness".

Mushin is when the mind is not full of emotions, sentiments, beliefs, thoughts etc. and as such, is linked with the universe as a whole. This is why it can be found at the core of martial arts philosophy.

Mushin is the mind-set when it is generated through the lack of ego. Indeed, it is not an empty mind like a shell is empty, but it refers to a mind that has freedom and is completely aware.

The notion of Mushin is associated with the Japanese representative phrase "mizu no kokoro", or in English, "mind like water". This psychological outlook presents an approach that is in complete unison with the universe and is similar to that of a calm body of water, where the surface mirrors a crystal clear image of the world around it, just as a mirror would do. Mushin is not something that can be attained mentally; it has to be felt. It is the ultimate understanding of the inner self. It takes one many years to attain Mushin.

William Miyagi

Satori

Instead of being an exceptional state of being, Satori is a concept where the individual goes back to the fundamental, pure form of the human mind.

Also referred to as Enlightenment, Satori is not a concept that can be realized through the mind. Instead, it is something that individuals must experience for themselves. When your body and mind are in unison with each other, it is only then that you will find the character of Satori.

Satori is there within us even prior to our births and animals have Satori at all times as they are in their own fundamental forms, constantly connected to the universe. It is humanity who longer possesses the pure form of consciousness.

As a result, humanity has to rediscover this pure form of Satori but do not think that Satori is some sort of achievement to be attained. Release everything, perform zazen and go about your day to day life. The more time you spend on overthinking how to achieve Satori then the more time you lose. Satori cannot be confined to mere words, it is something that cannot be limited by boundaries. Zen has no such boundaries. When you use the practice of zazen in the present moment, then you have Satori.

Chapter 5
How Meditation Fits In

"When you dig a well, there's no sign of water until you reach it, only rocks and dirt to move out of the way. You have removed enough; soon the pure water will flow," said Buddha." - Deepak Chopra

In the above quotation, Buddha refers to how to make water flow from seemingly dry land but it's symbolic of something else. In a world filled to brimming with thought and action, how can you find that perfect peace that helps you to understand life better? Just as in the above example, the workers had to move rocks and dirt, so too must you remove all the debris from within your mind. We all have the following thoughts going through our minds all the time. There's no wonder everything is so complicated:

- ✓ Past regrets
- ✓ Negative feelings and emotions

- ✓ Resentment
- ✓ Bad and good memories
- ✓ Data gleaned from work and life

No one can say they don't have some of this stored in their heads. Meditation helps you to get rid of the rocks so that symbolically the "water flows" or in fact you are able to see beyond all of the rocks or thoughts that are blocking your way to actually understanding. Meditation helps to concentrate the mind on different elements so that you are able to free the mind from the constraints that life puts on it. When practiced on a regular basis, this allows a clarity like you have never ever experienced in your life and it is this clarity that Gautama Buddha used to find the solution to all human suffering and it works. There is absolutely no doubt whatsoever that the solution he found is effective. This Zen state is a state where you are able to remove all of those rocks and see beyond them.

The process of meditation

You have several different methods open to you and these include Yoga Meditation, which you can learn with professional teachers if you wish, or you have breathing meditation, which is fairly simple to learn on your own. The advantage of a group session is that a guru or teacher may be able to correct your stance or explain the approach better than a layperson and thus people do gain a lot of inspiration from the interaction.

Meditation should always be undertaken in an area of calm. For instance, make sure that the TV or radio is turned off and that the place you choose is calm and quiet. You also need to know that you won't be interrupted during the process so should choose a time of day when you know this is more likely. Try and make it at a regular time so that you get into the habit because it's a good habit to have. You need to be dressed comfortably and to be seated during the process. You don't need to sit in complicated seated positions at this time because it's not about that. It's about meditation on a simple basis.

Sit in a chair, which allows you to have a straight back, and your head should be slightly raised to open up the air passages and make breathing much easier. Learn the process first and what is expected of you and then practice it.

The breathing process

Close your eyes to stop distractions. Breathe in through the nose and hold the breath, but while you are breathing in and out, count. Let the breath out through the nose. I always try to hold the breath for a moment inside me and then exhale from the abdomen. You may wonder what this breathing is all about. Well, it's not just about breathing. Do not think of anything except the breathing and the numbers. When you get to ten, go back to one again. If thoughts invade your mind, go back to one again. You should be thinking of nothing at all but the breathing.

How Meditation Helps

Meditation helps to give your mind a rest in simple terms, but it does so much more than that. It clears out all the cobwebs and it makes you much more able to see things clearly. This process of meditation is very helpful to you and you will find that it sharpens your instincts and that you are able to solve problems more easily. There is more to it as you get better at it, but if you are like me and have never done this before, then I want you to discover what else it does for you, because there is no doubt in my mind that you will and it's an amazing discovery. Practice this for about 20 minutes a day at first. You may think that sounds easy but try sitting without thinking for more than about 3 minutes and you will find it's a challenge. It's important for you to drop all thoughts while meditating so expect it to take practice.

Zen and Health

Zen mediation has a great number of benefits for us, not just in the mind and soul, but for the physical body as well. Through Zen meditation, you can enhance your physical and mental health.

Many people from all areas around the world have claimed that meditation has given them great benefits; there are countless stories from people of all cultures, backgrounds, education, ages, etc. who will state that meditation has not only given them great spiritual help, but mental help as well. Whilst the benefits of Zen meditation have been discussed and well known, it can go beyond just this notion.

Whilst the notion to have a healthy mind and spirit is something to be desired, possessing a healthy body is something to aspire to as well.

Reducing Anxiety and Stress

A number of medical studies and research surrounding the health benefits of meditation have been conducted in various countries, illustrating the fact that meditative practices stimulates the left pre-frontal cortex, whist at the same time, reducing movement in the right pre-frontal cortex of the brain.

Better Sleep and Rest Time

You will find yourself sleeping better, deeper and far more peacefully when you practice Zen meditation on a regular basis. Your body requires a good sleep pattern because when you sleep, your body repairs all the damage it has sustained throughout the previous day.

Improved Immune System

Previous medical studies performed have shown that Zen meditation aids in improving the body's natural immune system. If your immune system is good, then you will find that you don't get as ill and contract minor viruses and ailments such as sore throats, common colds and the flu for example.

Reduces Sensitivity to Pain

Let's face it, pain is not something to be enjoyed and through practicing Zen meditation on a day to day basis, you can reduce your sensitivity to pain. You won't lose the ability to actually feel pain but you will be taught how to effectively manage dealing with it much better through Zen meditation.

Slows Down the Aging Process

When you practice Zen meditation you teach your body how to slow down your body's rate of respiration so that it consumes less oxygen than before. The progression of the body's physical aging relies on how much oxygen you use; therefore, the less oxygen you use, the slower the progression of aging. You can do this by simply controlling your breathing.

Improved Blood Circulation

In addition to all the other benefits, your blood circulation is improved through Zen meditation, as well as lowering your heart rate. When this happens, your body looks healthier, your skin glows, your hair looks shinier and your nails look great. An improved blood circulation is well documented for having additional health benefits.

Mood and Behavior

When you are not under as much stress, you feel better in yourself and meditation can aid in reducing the occurrence of anxiety attacks. Meditation can help enhance the creation of serotonin, known as the happy emotion, which can help fight depression, insomnia, obesity, headaches and other ailments, which are all known to emerge if this chemical is not produced in sufficient amounts.

Improved Daily Posture

Most of us will experience pain from issues with our postures, especially when we are typically sitting in front of the computer, watching television or long periods of time driving a car. Since Zen meditation requires you to sit in a certain way, zazen actually helps you gain a better posture, allowing your back muscles to strengthen. Through this, your body will become healthier, stronger and far more tones since it aligns the spine and the surrounding muscles. Your abdominal muscles will become stronger, resulting in a good firm core. This, in turn, will safeguard your back from physical pains and aches. In addition to this, when you have good posture you look absolutely fantastic!

Addiction and Recovery

These days, it can be quite easy to become addicted to something, whether that is drugs, alcohol, and shopping, gambling or even food. Zen meditation can help you identify if you have an addiction as well as helping you beat them. Buddhism views addictions as an intense case of attachment – to panic, to defeat, to longing, nothingness, and no sense of purpose in life. Through Zen meditation you can defeat these fears and concentrate on finding what your life's meaning is, therefore treating the addiction.

Zen Meditation

Mindfulness

Zen is the practice of going about your normal everyday life but being aware of everything. It is extremely easy for us to perform our normal tasks on automated pilot and not really taking notice about what is actually going on or even what is running through our heads. Zen is about learning to experience every single moment in that single moment, without letting unnecessary fears, hopes, desires (or other illusionary aspects) stand in our way.

Those who practice Zen are aware of everything – what they see, what they touch, what they taste, what they hear and what they can smell. As a result, they are one with what they are doing. When they eat, they are concentrating on what they are eating and the act of eating; when they are practicing meditation they are allowing themselves to become one with the universe in that exact moment, without letting anything distract them, not even the notions of Enlightenment or the Buddha.

It is the Zen notion that what goes on in our heads is the natural occurrence of the mind and shouldn't be ceased, ignored or dismissed. Overthinking thoughts do occur but when that happens they should be pushed aside so that the mind is not burdened with fear, anxiety, hope and desires. When you free your mind of such a burden, then you relieve the mind of such suffering, allowing the cosmic truth to be exposed.

Stilling the Mind

The intention of Zen meditation is to allow the mind to cease its chaotic progression of unnecessary thoughts. As such, Zen meditation is often known as a way of "stilling the mind". There are several techniques in Zen Buddhism that are shown to people; these techniques have been established for centuries and are well known as effective methods.

You can practice Zen meditation by yourself or with a group of others. There are group retreats, known as a sesshin, where you can go and practice with others, allowing yourself to remember you are part of a big Buddhist society and part of the universe as a whole.

Zazen

Zazen is the main Zen Buddhist custom. This is where you will meditate in a variety of postures in order to open yourself up with the Buddha-nature. You will find that zazen is utilized in a variety of ways depending on which school you attend. For example, in Soto Zen you typically face a wall whereas you sit in a circle looking at everyone in Rinzai schools.

Posture

You can meditate in any position that allows your spine to remain in a somewhat straight line. You can sit on the floor, on a chair or even standing up. The most widely known posture in Zen meditation is referred to as the Lotus Position; this is where you sit with your left foot positioned on your right thigh and your right foot sits on your left thigh. However, this is quite an uncomfortable position for those new to Zen meditation. The Half Lotus, where one foot is positioned on top of the other thigh, is far more comfortable for novices, but you can also sit with your legs crossed or sit on your knees.

Methods of Meditation

You don't have to use elaborate methods in Zen meditation; simply by regulating your own breathing, just focusing on this, allows you to become one with your breathing. You can also meditate through reciting chants, focusing on a flame, and you don't even have to remain motionless. A lot of Zen practitioners use the walking meditation method.

Self-discipline

Let's face it, we all usually stop doing something because it doesn't hold our interest for very long, does it? With Zen meditation, you will learn how to keep going despite the boredom, despite numbness in the legs or even that you need the bathroom rather badly. You learn the art of self-discipline.

Koan Meditation

Koans are essentially questions, or even riddles, that help stimulate spiritual realization. Zen Buddhist masters will often ask their students these questions to educate or test them. They are not actually a goal, but instead as a tool in order to aid you in your understanding of the Buddha-nature, to enhance your perception of what is reality.

A famous koan is "In clapping both hands a sound is heard; what is the sound of one hand?"

What makes it annoying and difficult for Westerners dealing with koans is that despite studying long and hard, is the realization that there is no single right answer or response when faced with a koan. To complete a koan, one must detach oneself from all considerations and beliefs to reply unthinkingly. For Westerners, it is generally taught that there is a right answer to use with all questions, which isn't applicable in the East. In addition to this, koans cannot be solved simply through learning scriptures by heart or receiving clarification from the teacher. The simplest way of solving a koan is by conversing with a master otherwise you are simply not going to be able to do so otherwise.

The earliest compilation of koans is dated back to the 11th century and is frequently used in the Rinzai School.

Zen and the Japanese Arts

Not long after Zen Buddhism emerged in ancient Japan, the school began to have a deep effect on how Japanese culture progressed and ultimately was incorporated in the country's religious and aesthetic establishment.

Through the traditions of numerous arts in Japan, various ethical and religious thoughts and beliefs progressed through the country and into the mainstream education. When Japan had cut itself off from the rest of the world and isolated itself, these various artistic traditions evolved in a manner that is quintessentially Japanese, with many of these incorporating elements from Zen Buddhism.

Spiritual Disciplines

Every single artistic tradition in Japan, including the chado tea ceremony, the flower arrangement practice known as ikebana, martial arts and shodo (the art of calligraphy), were all affected by aspects of Zen Buddhism customs. They were then changed into a spiritual subject that concentrated on stillness, easiness and self-growth.

In Japan there is an age-old custom where one can learn about art, not just for its own sake, but also for religious means. When combining this with Zen beliefs, art can be an especially tranquil journey and allowing one's self to learn about the inner self, which results in concentration, tranquility and learning to be calm. Educating oneself on art with Zen principles combined, concentrates on how important it is for the mind and the body to become one in order to master all the arts. When you create art combined with a Zen outlook, then the mind allows you to push aside the dark veil of illusion and see clearly.

It is quite likely that the Japanese art scene would never have progressed to its current heights without the influence of Zen Buddhism to guide it along its path.

Zen Aesthetic or Wabi-sabi

Although Zen Buddhism was essentially transported to Japan from China, the embellishment and refinement of its central subject is extremely different to the Chinese notions of beauty. There is a distinctive quality to Zen Buddhism that the Chinese sects didn't possess, including an admiration for self-control, irregularity, defectiveness, rusticity and the natural pure state.

This Zen notion is commonly referred to as Wabi-sabi, and it sees the true beauty in everything even if it is not perfect, permanent or even not complete. We see the concept of Wabi-sabi in artworks, where the concept is portrayed in quite a modest manner. It is quite a natural quality to view in art and there is a strong affiliation with nature in arts using Wabi-sabi. This concept has been the source of inspiration for countless Japanese artists in all genres throughout the long centuries and is even used by painters, sculptors and poets even in modern times.

Harmony with Nature

It is easy to see that Japanese culture and society possesses a strong relationship with nature. This type of relationship is one of the key values in Shintoism, the native Japanese religion that existed long before Buddhism arrived onto the scene. This value has been expanded and the meaning has been deepened through Zen Buddhism.

Zen Buddhism sees nature as a manifestation of the sacred. Zen Buddhism does not seek to control or guide or even manage it; instead, Zen creates a strong spiritual relationship with nature. This can easily be seen through the different artistic forms in the country and especially recognizable in Zen gardens.

Even today, the Japanese people respect nature. It is well known that one must have this harmonious relationship with nature so that the Zen principles can thrive. When nature succeeds then humanity and nature can live in harmony, each one welcoming of the other.

You will find though that you will get better at it with persistence.

William Miyagi

Chapter 6
Mindfulness

"You are the community now. Be a lamp for yourselves. Be your own refuge. Seek for no other. All things must pass. Strive on diligently. Don't give up." – Gautama Buddha

One of the most useful exercises I found to make me more mindful was to climb up to a beauty spot that I know where I am so close to nature that it overwhelms me. This is my inspirational place and reminds me of how small I am in the order of things. The Buddha says, "Be your own refuge" and he's quite right. In this place, far above the moorland, I can see nature at its best and find an inner strength that acts as my refuge by visiting this place to remind me of how small I am. Why would I want to do that? Let me explain.

William Miyagi

If you choose a spot where there's going to be a great sunset, and which is awe inspiring, you get closer to your belief system than you can imagine. It doesn't matter who your God is. It doesn't matter what race you are. In this space in time, you know that you are just a small pebble on a beach, but it's a really comforting thought. Your awareness and your senses tell you that being humble is a wonderful thing. When you can recognize humility, you actually enrich your life because it changes your attitude toward everything. In this place, I am able to be aware of the vastness of the world. I am also able to see how all of the small elements that I see come together to make a vast whole, and I am part of that whole. Thus, although I am small, I am as vital to the scene as the tree on the ridge over there, or the little bit of redness that's starting to show in the sky.

When you learn how to feel humble, you also learn how to be very appreciative in life. You tend to notice things more. This morning, for example, I noticed dewdrops on the grass. I stopped to look at them and watched one roll down a leaf. I then walked down the woodland and noticed the forest floor. Flowers were starting and the water at the bottom of the garden is running faster than usual but very clear. In fact, I could see fish and I could discern the colors of pebbles within the water.

People who are not mindful don't notice all of the things that are there in life to be embraced. Whatever you learned about multi-tasking didn't come from any Zen teaching because Zen teaches you to do every task and be mindful of it. Drink your coffee in small sips and enjoy the flavor, rather than rushing for another cup. Taste your cereals and distinguish the different textures and tastes as you eat. Take your time.

The world is a very rushed place and people who multi-task think that they are so clever, but how can you do all of those jobs properly if you don't use your mind to concentrate on any one in particular? Short term, it may work, but mindfulness works every time and helps you to find answers to problems, helps you to appreciate the world in which you live and helps you to see the bigger picture that multi-tasking people will never see. That's the difference.

If you can incorporate mindfulness into your life, you live in a better way, you are conscious of what you eat, of what you say, of how you react to any given circumstances and with this mindfulness comes a greater understanding. People who are mindful don't shout at others. They don't feel negative thoughts because they don't allow themselves to. Negative thoughts all add to the confusion of life and they are not necessary. If you feel angry with someone, you make yourself suffer. If you feel jealous, it's you who suffers too, so you need to find a way within your mindfulness to stop a while and let Zen kick in and negative thoughts go. Forgive people that hurt you. Let it be their problem to sort out. Let go of resentment. It serves no purpose. Be aware at all times of the way you feel toward the world and mindfulness of everything around you won't leave much room for negativity. You will find you are enchanted by what you see and surprised by what you didn't notice in the past.

The road through life is actually very simple and yet people kick over the stepping stones looking for more complex answers. They send ripples through the waters of life trying to uncover solutions when the stepping stones themselves already present the solutions. Thus, if you let go of this pointless search for any kind of justification for why people act in the way they do, and concentrate on your own Zen, the water is still and the stepping stones that lead you from one area of your life to the next are solid footholds.

Siddhartha Gautama found that the obvious was there before his eyes but that life's confusion stops most people from ever seeing it. We put up barriers. We complicate things because we are taught from a very young age to brainstorm and in brainstorming, we are also expected to look at alternatives, add things up – take into account society's view of something and still come up with solutions. The solution is already there and you disturb the waters digging so deep. You really don't need to. It's the stuff that heart attacks are made of and yet people hold onto the preconceptions that they need to put themselves through so much torture in their lives to find answers. Answers are found in meditation and in mindfulness. Put these two together and the answers come without even having to ask. That's what Zen is all about and when you practice it, it is life changing.

William Miyagi

Conclusion

I am sitting in the sunshine. The rays of light that are pouring down on me are heaven sent. After a winter of discontent, it's enjoyable to notice everything happening around me. The birds are in full song. The Acer in the garden is a beautiful shade of golden green and the skies are looking hopeful of a day without rain.

How is this relevant? It's relevant because mindfulness is that takes away all those negative thoughts. I don't simply wake up and look to see if it's raining. There's much more to see than that and Zen allows me to see it. The water lilies on the pond hide overnight and only come out when the sun shines. The rose buds need deadheading. This is how simple life is. I am hungry and need to eat something to give me energy. From the trees in the summer months, I will be able to taste the nectar of the delicious golden plums that are now hanging from each branch in small groups of green promising a summer of thirst quenching glory.

Why am I talking about my garden? The answer is because it gives me a sense of peace. Your peace may be in looking across the water on the coastline. Your peace may be found sitting in a city park feeding the ducks. It won't be found in the land of worries and unhappiness. It won't be found in anger, resentment, jealousy or greed. It won't be found in the argument you just had with your boss or the anger you felt toward the driver in front of you who made a mistake. Let go of these things and you make room for so much more than that, and your life is worth it.

Zen allows you to do that. Learn to be humble. If the driver in front of you made a mistake, they probably regret it much more than you do. Be humble; show empathy because they have to live with their mistakes just as you have to live with yours. Adding your anger to their error makes it even more difficult for another human being when understanding that people make mistakes is so much simpler.

The boss who upsets you probably does it because he knows it upsets you. Zen takes away the need to belittle others, but it should also show you the way to see that the problem is his, not yours and empathy toward him works better than responding with anger. When you empathize, you stop negativity in its tracks, because you give anger and negativity no place to go.

I hope that this book has imparted information that will help you, as a new Zen practitioner to make the most of the time that you have on this Earth and to appraise the way that you let all the things around you change who you are. Meditation helps you considerably because it helps you to see more clearly your part in this universe and to establish that you want it to be a positive presence, rather than one that causes strife and difficulty. Once you simplify your approach using the four truths as your guide and the eight fold path as your chosen route, you will have unlocked the secret to peace, harmony and inner strength and you may find that you also get one step further toward enlightenment.

William Miyagi

Printed in Great Britain
by Amazon.co.uk, Ltd.,
Marston Gate.